Please read this book now, before you do anything else

You feel as bad as it's possible to feel right now.

Maybe it's the first time you've felt this way, maybe you get these feelings a lot. Either way, you're thinking there's no alternative to killing yourself.

But you're wrong.

Although it's hard for you to believe, there is another way to cope with your pain and hopelessness. A way that hurts less, and works better at helping you start to feel good.

This book is about that other way – what it is and how to make it work.

It gives you some tips on staying alive – even when you might not want to. And it also helps you imagine your life when you start to feel good again – because you *will*.

Let's start by talking about the better way to ease your pain.

SUICIDE LASTS FOR EVER

Your problem doesn't

You won't always feel like this

Suicide works. It's a permanent way to stop feeling bad.

But it also stops you ever feeling good, or loved, or proud, or special, or elated, or curious, or giggly, or surprised, or warm, or sexy.

Time is also a cure for feeling bad, but it works differently. It stops the pain more slowly, but it doesn't stop you feeling all those other things, all through the rest of your life.

It's like this:

Suicide kills all feelings, good and bad, for ever.

Time kills bad feelings too, but it also lets you keep the good ones. For ever.

But does choosing time really work?

Well, yes it does, so long as you use it the right way and fill it with the right things.

This book is about how to do that, so that you can start to feel OK again.

HOW TO GIVE TIME A CHANCE TO WORK

Use it the right way and fill it with the right things

Start with talking.

Talk to a friend, a parent, a partner, a colleague or a teacher about how you feel. Do it now. Talk about how dark and hopeless everything seems to you at the moment.

Ring your doctor, go to A & E. Ring NHS 24 (Scotland 0845 4 242424) or NHS Direct (England 0845 4647). Ask someone else to get help for you or call the Samaritans on 08457 909090 straight away.

The aim of talking is to get treatment and support. Your friend, teacher or family member will organise it when they know how bad you feel. Your doctor, the NHS or the Samaritans can help get support and treatment.

Keep talking to people 'till you find someone who can help.

Don't stop talking. Talking gets you the support you need.

What else can you do to fill time with?
Turn Over.

MORE WAYS TO USE TIME

Walking

If it's daylight, go outside and walk quickly, until you feel tired. Walk quite quickly, as if you're on the way to somewhere (you are, you're on the way to feeling better). Even better, walk with a friend and talk about good times or anything that grabs you.

Look at the buildings and trees around you. Look up at the sky. Listen for birds. Count how many buses or trucks you see or count your own steps so that bad thoughts don't go round and round in your head.

Eating

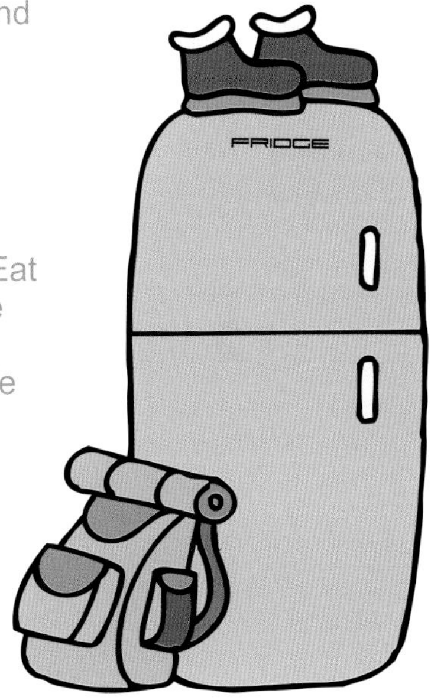

Raid the fridge, go to the shop. Eat something and try to taste all the flavours. Don't drink alcohol, it'll make you feel worse after a while and you may get so drunk you lose it.

Food helps you feel better because it gives you the energy you need to recover.

If you have an eating problem and food just turns you off, still try to eat regularly, even if it's not much. Basic stuff like sandwiches are fine, though if you like to cook, this is a time to do more of it.

EVEN MORE WAYS TO FILL TIME

Watching

Go to the pictures, go to the match, get a DVD out – and do it with a friend if you can. Go to the park and watch people running, skating or playing games.

Some of them felt like you only last week.

Seeing

Try to see things from a new angle. Instead of focusing on what's gone wrong and how bad you feel, move your mind to different things. Make a list of all the positive stuff in your life, now and in the past.

Include things like friends, things you've learned to do well (like swimming, riding a bike, driving a car), happy times you've had on holiday.

Write down 5 things you're grateful for – the fact that you're not starving, you have warm clothing, the blossom looks great in Spring...like that.

WALKING?
EATING?

I don't feel like doing any of it!

Force yourself, just this once

Doing something, anything, is important. It fills time and helps create good feelings. Exercise really helps when you're feeling down, especially if you walk or run fast enough to get out of breath.

Getting jobs done also makes you feel better. Room a mess? Tidy it up a bit. Self a mess? Get up, have a shower and clean your teeth. Clothes in a smelly pile? Give them a wash. Car or bike need cleaning up? Do it. And when you're done, give yourself a pat on the back.

Try it – even if it's just for five minutes. Filling time with talking, walking, eating, watching and seeing helps it to work its magic and starts to take away the bad feelings.

Now here's what not to do.

DON'T SPEND TIME THINKING OR DRINKING

Break the circle of upsetting thinking

When you feel really down, sitting and thinking about it all by yourself makes you feel worse. It's like a vicious circle:

Feeling bad makes you have bad, hopeless thoughts.

Bad, hopeless thoughts make you feel even worse.

You feel even worse, so you have even more bad, hopeless thoughts.

The trick is to break the circle and start doing things. But don't drink alcohol.

Alcohol can ease the pain – for a short time. But then it makes it worse. You get a hangover and you probably look in your pocket the morning after and wonder where all your money went.

Drinking a lot of alcohol might seem like a way to forget your troubles, but people who get really drunk take risks, make mistakes and do stupid things.

MORE STUFF TO AVOID

No Cutting

Maybe you feel a sense of relief when you cut yourself. All the bad feelings come out with a rush and you feel better for a while. For some people, self-harm is the only way to make others understand how terrible they feel.

But cutting can go wrong. You could damage your nerves, leave ugly scars, get infected or, of course, slip up and really kill yourself

No Pushing

Don't push people away. When you feel down, you sometimes don't feel like bothering with people. But people are the way to get help and support. Even if you don't feel like it, let them in.

They'll understand what you're going through much better if you talk to them about it.

No Surfing

Chat rooms and online forums can also seem like an answer at first.

You connect with people like yourself, who may have been suicidal themselves. Trouble is, some websites talk as if suicide is the right response when you feel really down. If you reach one of these, log off straight away and never go back.

IT'S ALL ABOUT HOPE

There is a way out of that blind alley

Hopelessness kills.

When you feel hopeless you can't see a future – can't see the point of carrying on. It blinds you to the possibility of change.

How can you start to hope again? Trust yourself. Trust yourself to stick with the ideas in this book, to keep talking to other people, and to choose time instead of death.

Remember, time works better than suicide – all you have to do is use it the right way and fill it with the right things.

You can put up with anything if you know it won't last forever.

WHAT SETS OFF YOUR HOPELESS FEELINGS?

Most people find it hard to pinpoint why they feel bad, but time helps them feel better. Some people are different and can point to one big reason for their desperate feelings. If this is you, read this page.

A person?

Is someone bullying or threatening you? Are you in an abusive relationship at home, at school or at work? You can do something about it. Call one of these numbers now:
Domestic Violence: **0808 2000 247**
Bullying: **020 8554 9004 (Supportline)**
or **0800 1111 (Child line)**

A problem?

Homeless? Out of work? Behind on your payments? Struggling with sexuality? Call one of these numbers now: Homeless, call **Shelter** on **0808 800 4444** Out of work, call **Jobcentre Plus** on **0845 6060 234** In debt, call **Consumer Credit Counselling Service** on **0800 138 1111** Sexuality issues, call **The Samaritans** on **08457 909090**

A pattern?

Do you drink too much? Can't seem to keep a relationship? Take drugs? Binge on food? Call one of these numbers now: Drugs, including alcohol – call **Frank** on **0800 776600** Eating disorders, call **b-eat** on **0845 634 1414**. And ask your doctor if counselling could help.

YES, BUT...

I've heard all this stuff before and it doesn't do any good. Don't you think I'd have sorted myself out by now if anything actually worked?

How often do you say that?

Do you say it a lot, when people try to help?

Well, here's the thing - the more you say it, the worse you get, because 'Yes, but' stops you trying anything new.

Will you try an experiment for us? For the next two days, will you try not to say 'Yes, but' when someone suggests something? Instead, will you please say 'What if?'

What if it worked this time?

What if I felt better this time?

What if this is an answer?

What if this person really knows what they're talking about?

What if I'm wrong after all?

What if I believe them this time?

What if calling this number will get some help?

What if they're right and I **will** feel better in time?

ARE YOU TOO ASHAMED TO ASK FOR HELP?

Don't die of embarrassment

Keeping quiet about how you feel just makes it worse.

If you feel too ashamed or embarrassed to talk about your feelings, or if you believe that people will think you're pathetic or silly for feeling bad, you're wrong.

Almost everyone has been in a bad place at some time. You'd be surprised how many other people have felt as bad as you.

When someone ends their own life, the most common thing that's said by the people left behind is "If only we'd known it was that bad."

Don't die because you didn't want to be any trouble. Asking for help doesn't mean you're weak, it means you're human.

Go to someone you trust right now and say "Help me". They will.

YOU'RE NOT THE ONLY ONE WHO DIES

When you killed yourself, you killed me, too. There are no colours any more, everything is grey and hopeless.

I know you felt the same way – that's why you ended it. But you didn't end the sadness, you gave it to me.

Is that how it works? Do people who kill themselves just hand their hurt and hopelessness to those they leave behind?

I feel so bad that I failed you and let you down. Parents are supposed to protect their children and I messed up.

I wish I could have written a letter like this to you before you died, to make you understand that you weren't by yourself and had me on your side.

All you had to do was talk to me, you know. Tell me how bad you felt. Shout and scream at me if necessary and I would have got you some help. God knows how, but I would have done anything.

We were having a real laugh just yesterday. Now you're gone. You'd have got over what they said – they were just picking on anyone – it wasn't about you. Why did you do that. I feel so angry with you – and so sad.

I have been off school because of this but I would rather go to school and you be alive so that you can call me names again and help me with homework.

Now sharpen your pencil.
You've got a job to do.

WRITE YOUR LIFE STORY

Imagine what you'd do if you didn't end it all

Imagine your future on the next two pages. Don't write the story so far, think what might happen in the rest of your life and write that down instead.

Don't hold back or settle for ordinary things. If you reckon you could be Prime Minister, write it down! If you want to have five children, decide their names! If you're going to be a film star, an author, a doctor, a musician or a centre forward, say so!

When you've written your future, keep it and look over it from time to time. Cross things out and change them over the weeks and months – nobody gets it right first time and anyway, you might change your mind about all those kids.

My life from now on...

This is your future. Don't throw it away.

THE END

SUICIDE

STOPS
EVERYTHING

YOU'LL NEVER FEEL
BAD AGAIN

YOU'LL NEVER FEEL
GOOD AGAIN

YOU'LL NEVER FEEL
ANYTHING AGAIN

BUT YOUR FRIENDS
AND FAMILY WILL FEEL
AWFUL FOREVER

THE BEGINNING

STAYING ALIVE

IT'S LIKE
STARTING AGAIN

START TO FIX
FEELING BAD

STARTING TO FEEL GOOD

STARTING TO FEEL NEW
THINGS ALL YOUR LIFE

STARTING TO MEET NEW
PEOPLE AND GET EVEN
CLOSER TO THE PEOPLE
YOU LOVE

DON'T JUST SIT THERE, TALK TO SOMEONE

Don't be alone

If you feel suicidal, talk to someone NOW and explain how bad you feel.

Don't be embarrassed, don't be angry, don't die because you didn't want to be any trouble.

Time is a better solution than suicide, but you must use it the right way and fill it with the right things to feel hopeful again.

Talk to a parent, friend, partner or teacher about how you feel. Tell him or her how dark and hopeless everything seems to you at the moment.

Ring your doctor, go to A&E, ring NHS Direct, NHS 24 or the Samaritans straight away.

All the numbers you need are over the page.

NUMBERS THAT WILL GET YOU HELP

Write your doctor's name and number down here

....

....

....

Not got a doctor? Visit **www.yell.com** and search for doctors near where you live

24 hour telephone help:

NHS 24 (Scotland) **0845 4 242424**
www.nhs24.com

NHS Direct (England & Wales) **0845 4647**
www.nhsdirect.nhs.uk

Breathing Space (Scotland): **0800 838587**
www.breathingspacescotland.co.uk

Samaritans: **08457 909090**
www.samaritans.org jo@samaritans.org,
or write a letter to Chris, P.O. Box 90,
Stirling FK8 2SA

Domestic violence: **0808 2000 247**
www.womensaid.org.uk

Bullying: **020 8554 9004** (Supportline)

Childline: **0800 1111** www.nspcc.org.uk

Eating disorders: Beat **0845 634 1414**
www.b-eat.co.uk help@b-eat.co.uk

MORE CONTACTS FOR INFORMATION & SUPPORT

Anxiety

National Phobics Society:
08444 775 774 (9.15-9pm)
www.phobics-society.org.uk
or email info@phobics-society.org.uk
Triumph over Phobia: www.topuk.org

Depression

Action on Drepession:
0808 802 2020
www.actionondepression.org
info@actionondepression.org

General mental health

Mind info line: **0845 7660163**
www.mind.org.uk

Ask your doctor or social services about other resources

Don't stop talking.
Talking gets you support and treatment.